Armadillo Charm

by Carlos Cumpián

TIA CHUCHA PRESS
CHICAGO

Acknowledgments

Some of the poems have appeared or are scheduled to appear in the following publications (sometimes in versions different from those collected here): ACM *Another Chicago Magazine*; *Howling Dog: a Journal of Letters, Lines, and Words*; *ViAztlan: a Journal of Arts and Letters*; *New Chicana/Chicano Writing*; *Dark Night Field Notes*; *Riverwest Review*; *Repuesta Xicana Anthology*.

My gracias goes out to those who have supported and inspired me during the years these were written: the humble hearts in each sweat lodge praying to the Spirit for health, help, and peace. Abrazos to the daring points of our literary spear; Ana Castillo, Sandra Cisneros, Dee Sweet, Luis J. Rodriguez, Martín Espada, Adrian C. Louis, Michael Warr, José Montoya, Li-Young Lee, Achy Obejas, Clayton Eshleman, M.L. Liebler, Mort Castle, Barry Silesky, Marc Zimmerman, these are the reflecting pools who made me look; Miriam Berkeley, Virginia Boyle, Diana Solis, Kim Johnson, Mary Hawley, Robert Lifson, Raúl Niño, J. Ingrid Lesley, los members y amigos del Woodland Pattern, Guild Complex, The Guadalupe Arts Center, Tres Américas, Mexican Fine Arts Center Museum, Movimiento Artístico Chicano and my ultimate editor and dance partner–Cynthia Gallaher.

Printed in the United States of America

ISBN 1-882688-09-0
Library of Congress Number: 96-60120

Book design: Jane Brunette
Cover drawing: Camilo Cumpián
Photo: Robert Lifson

PUBLISHED BY:
TIA CHUCHA PRESS
A Project of the Guild Complex
PO Box 476969
Chicago, IL 60647

DISTRIBUTED BY:
NORTHWESTERN UNIVERSITY PRESS
Chicago Distribution Center
11030 S. Langley
Chicago, IL 60628

Funding for this project was partially provided by the National Endowment for the Arts, the Illinois Arts Council, and the Lannan Foundation.

For those who love the earth.

Table of Contents

Armadillo Charm

I.
Armadillos are flattened on roads every week,
ending up like some cold drunk Indians
who lie down on warm dark asphalt after
trips back from fiery-watering holes.

Smart armadillos amble jobless,
happy not to work in a zoo, they stroll
plush river grass and smooth red pebble paths,
far from fast two-legged foreigners.

II.
Armadillos want to be around when the earth smears
the last mad zigzag road from her body,
armadillos are patient, armadillos count
every wind stir roaring off solar coasters,
bringing layers of fine star dandruff to land,
that's why they look like dried-up
sailors or the last face of thirsty travelers,
armadillos are prone to tropical leprosy,
like lost botanists they go skinning themselves
raw while roaming hungry in the dark.

Before the sky master tossed sparks to bake all creation
with telltale universal panther carbon, nothing big had died
yet, truly a nadir niche for four-legged fossils, though not too
bad for fishes, it nearly killed calorie-starved armadillo.

III.
Armadillo, ugly craggy creature, with twenty tribes
        across the hemisphere,
armadillo, with few friends from beginning to end:
the hairy tree sloth, and rapacious ant eater,
each claiming to be his pal, sharing a pre-Ice-Age pedigree
with the armored rascal, each sticking to the same survival
diet since making the Paleocene,
peg-tooth armadillo got hot under his sixty million year-old
scapular collar and became a cranium-hard tourist walking backwards–
going south to north, before entering borderland Texas.

Gringos discovered Armadillo in the mid-nineteenth century,
the indigenous people had always known him,
but history started with the newcomers ripe for independence,
Alamo insurance, Austin honky-tonks, accordion *conjunto*-polka suds,
salsa music, blue-eyed Baptists, plastic saints on dashboards,
chile-flavored beans and King Ranch cowboys trained by *vaqueros*,
raised on tacos of onion-soaked armadillo,
available only in south *Texaztlan*,
giving the chicken-colored meat cult status.

IV.
Armadillos are fond of colorful flowers, thorns pose no problem,
and armadillos love dark dirt body bugs, slugs and worms
on steamy leaves and bright powdery pistils-to-petals.
There are no obese armadillos.
Armadillo has no patent on this diet, so some of us
wanting to slim down just might like to try it. You go first.

Armadillo kitsch means being flayed for book ends, salt shakers or
decorative baskets to please some schmucks passing through airports,
armadillos become rustic *canastas* filled with pecans and
pomegranates after eyes are shredded by twenty-two caliber bullets,
there's no graveside music for their passing,

no lead-lined casket for a charade with eternity,
not a moment of ritual magic,
nothing cushions armadillo death when shells, cars or trucks
splatter red guts like gastral litter on subtropical scrublands.

V.
Armadillo prefers his original name in Nahuatl, *Ayotochtli*,
a combination of turtle and rabbit,
looking like a hedgehog in an obsidian helmet,
sturdy enough to become an instrument,
complete with strings for *charango*-mountain music,
Ayotochtli, Ayotochtli, Ayotochtli,

"Ah, don't touch me," he seems to say,
balling up after he burrows away
at speeds pushing fifty,
armadillos have lived like charmed moving stones
for generations, so don't knickknack them to extinction,
be compassionate compadres,
adopt one.

We Don't Wanna Peso Much

"Let's make this Thanksgiving completely different,"
some big shot musta' said, on a slow news day
full of state-wide layoffs and wallet-bruising deficits,
"Let's privatize the immigration department
and allow every patriot to become a migra agent.
Rush this idea over the airwaves,
Lord knows we need more involved voters."

Meanwhile, fiery-eyed *Superbarrio*
in front of his tiny tele in Tenochtitlan,
watches helplessly as the U.S. Border Patrol
and National Guard units seal off the roads
leading to occupied México, home of the real Pep Boys.

"The turkeys finally got their way,
though both sides will suffer when it's over,
no one is getting through Tijuana/San Diego,
Juárez/El Paso, the two Laredos or even
Piedras Negras/Eagle Pass without a hassle,
every ride is stopped twenty minutes of the river,
often it's an hour before you can either drive ahead
or expect to be dragged away in chains,
instead of heading off free toward Arizona, California,
New Mexico, and Texas. Now they got an army of troopers busy
twisting concertina wire and singing, 'Light up the border,'
while blabbing about new Blazers, baseball pennants,
and burritos as big as their heads chased by beer
colder than an Alaskan whore's bed."

Superbarrio from miles away can hear the gabas say,
"Just where are those busboys, dishwashers and cooks?
Got any idea where the gardeners and groundskeepers are hiding?
We can't make Mexican food without the ingredients or from a book,
has anyone seen Armando, Mario, Justo or Beto?
Those guys should be here by now, filling bags of groceries.
Mr. Franklin, we got a ton of letters to get out this week, and
Irma, Maria, Luz and the new girl from Michoacán didn't come in.
Kind of quiet in the barrio for a Saturday night, ain't it
        Sergeant O'Malley?
Last week my school bus was half empty.
        What happened to the Latino kids,
they all started eating Jimson weed or something?"

From burning beaches where ice blue raspas are shaved into cones,
to the dark apple orchards after the fall dumps its lonely pickers,
to the gravel pits of sorrow, where ruined bruised backs
        once gathered,
is there no one conducting an underground railroad to save targeted
people, who lack the empire's proper papers for staying this side
        of the fence.

Black and white Los Angeles rejects
millions of dollars in sales and taxes,
handing over to soldiers an entire football stadium of
        Spanish-speakers,
the radio warns, "A battalion of barrio Brown Berets are blocking
all roads to East L.A.," and what's worse Los Lobos canceled
        their concert.

"Good morning, did you hear the Gov has ordered extra police
helicopters to flank suburban commuters headed downtown.
This is live drive-time talk radio with Richard Byrd,
we're taking your calls on the immigration troubles."

"Hello, this is Herb, all I'm saying is we Anglos are sick and tired
of the sneaky Mexican take over. Back in 1992, that writer guy,
          Carlos Fuentees,
bragged on PBS how Mexican women are like Trojan Horses
          bringing in their bellies new partisans
for their slow demographic reconquest of the American Southwest. "

"Herb, sounds like you're worried about white folks'
zero population growth and losing your parking
space to a guy named Pancho buying his kid pampers."

"Hey, think what you want Dickey-bird,
the Mexies are pushing
for a permanent shift in our values,
and I'll guarantee it's about more than greasy menudo, corn-on-the-cob
sold as elotes, and tacos full of green runny nopales. You want your kids
          growing up eating all that?
 Look, they want to take back all our golf courses."

"Let's take another call, this time from Dallas.
          Hi Jack, what's on your mind?"

"Dickey, I'm calling on a cellular phone, it's hard to hear your show
from this grassy knoll because of the snipers.
Let me call you back later, to explain myself after all's well."
(click)

Juan ate seven slices of pizza (delivered by his illegal primo),
Juan ate seven hot hamburgers (served at minimum wages),
Juan ate seven heads of lettuce (sprayed with poisonous pesticides),
Juan ate seven sun-ripe tomatoes (with turtle-shell durability),
Juan ate seven bowls of corn flakes (a gift from the Hopis),
Juan ate seven hard-boiled eggs (someone crack a window),
Juan ate seven sour dough loaves (made by gay Frisco bakers),

Juan ate seven buttery pancakes (git yr own syrup, I ain't ja mama),
Juan ate seven bags of zoo peanuts
        (Animal Liberationists freed the monkeys),
Juan ate seven rolls of Californian sushi
        (green wasabe hotter than hades).

Juan will be eating the fruits of his labor when *la migra*
deports him out of the state that tilts to the ocean,
oyes Juan as they proposition you to leave,
diles que ya es muy tarde, it's already too late,
Chicago has been renamed *Chicano*, Illinois,
y la majority of *Americanos* use
more hot salsa *que* ketchup,
in fact tortillas are overtaking space
once reserved for white sliced bread,
while Spanish songs sink roots inside 35 million heads.

Juan, after you're safely across the border,
ten cuidado con ese gordito el media freak *Superbarrio*,
Mexico's masked righter of wrongs
(no relation to *subcomandante Marcos*)
is going to greet you and hold your trembling *mano*,
to pose for *fotos en La Jornada, Uno Más Uno y tal vez*
High Performance, pero tú sabes, it's going to take more than
a December pilgrimage to *nuestra Tonantzin-Guadalupe* or
any one woman or man in a flabby wrestler's mask and outfit
to prevent greedy Kens and Barbies
from La Jolla to Mount Shasta from attacking
the weakest immigrant links in
America's chain of command.

When Jesus Walked

"You don't wanna die like Crow McDonald, do ya?"
My cousin just shook his dark bushy hair,
took another beer and tossed his jean jacket on a chair.

I was talking 'bout Crow, a tall hook-nose peddler
in a black leather cabretta and jeans, who flew face first
into a soda delivery truck outside of Ragos food shop,
the truck's red and white logo branding his
beer-soaked brain.

Crow's casket was draped with biker colors while
ganja laughter closed the lid on that cold day,
six feet under, after a Chicago Outlaw's funeral.

Weeks later on a sleepy Sunday afternoon
I struggled to stay awake, and asked in a daze,
"Cuz, you used ta be an altar boy.
Think there's something in the incense that makes
people slower before dinner and Disney?"
"I wouldn't know, I haven't been to church in years,"
he replied. Then I drifted off and dreamt of Crow's
bony arms all folded up like wings as he said,
"Caw caw, I'm doing fine," and disappeared into the egg of darkness.

Waking up I sing, "We got to get up off this couch
        and find someone with a car.
See ya later Mom, I'll be back around eight."

Then who pulls up in his daddy's white Cadillac—Italian Tony,
with music pulsating the plush-padded interior,
we hop in and take a quick spin,
seven guys filling front and back seats,
it's so crowded we had no need for restraints, with our bony
shoulders pinned against each other, we bobbed ridiculously
to each tune, until fuzzy-haired Charlie Olsen squeaked,
"Let me out at 111th and the Ave,
I want to get somethin' to eat. . ."
Bye to the guy whose cremated parents
were kept at home in two rice-colored jars.

We drove on to find something
to smoke at Finchum's West Pullman pad,
after ten minutes of knocking, we agreed,
nothing could rouse Finchum from his lair,
if he was inside, he must've been out cold.
"Nah, I called him yesterday," Larry claimed,
"Said he's been wide awake for days on speed
reading books, The Idiot and The Stranger.
Weird, I can hear some mumbling, but there's no answer."

Under late September's autumnal rays
car windows rolled up, I clapped to full-throated
rock gospel on the car's radio,
"O happy days, when Jesus walked, O, when He walked."
In contrast my companions sat, stoned grass-eyed mystics.

Pausing at a four corner stop in a residential block,
normally as uneventful as changing a channel,
we philosophers at leisure missed
the pale blue transparent flashes
that grew bigger as it bounced
off a parked car's window,

too late,
we rolled out
to be struck broadside
by speeding Chicago cops,
Tony's daddy's caddy wavered,
then flipped onto its side,
as the song echoed the chorus.

Each shaggy head emerged from that tycoon's chariot
with the grave spoor of fear
mixed with the hashish breath
that greeted the huckleberries
as they peered in and asked,
"You ladies alright?" Hell, they changed their tunes
as soon as they saw Blackie's and Tom's mustaches,
while the rest of us held the unblinking golden
stare of the zig-zag rolling papers man,
before we heard,
"You're all under arrest, climb out
and assume the position,"
mixed with the radio's blissful,
"O, when Jesus walked, He took my pains away."

Before the Great Gorge

She raised the oven's temperature,
he unpeeled the plump poultry
from its factory plastic wrap,
they chopped onion, garlic, celery,
poured teaspoons of salt and sage,
stirred together ground black pepper
green parsley, a moon of dry bread to expand
beneath steaming giblet broth, as the round
dining table sprouted silver knives, forks and spoons.

Back during Squanto's time, wild bird meat simmered
            with acorn stuffing
and hot honey pumpkin
            joined sweet yams in bright buttery optimism,
releasing great appetites among Pilgrims
            in the new Massachusetts' air.

No parade of football mascots' sportsbabble
had spread like unbelted American waistlines.
But even then, bald babies and tipsy husbands
took satisfied afternoon naps,
while tired women did all the work.

Squanto's great, great, great, great grandchildren
take Thanksgiving in stride, drink cokes, coffee or beer
after finishing tonight's meal made from reservation deer,
someone offers fat and meat scraps to backyard dogs, another clears
the table as three sisters talk about finding work before Christmas,

cars fill up to drive mothers, uncles, aunties and cousins home,
teenagers smoke cigarettes, their words cloud around school,
past due assignments, and basketball,
no one speaks of the dark Dutch
or English sailing ships that landed
on these shores long ago or pale-eyed captains conquering
a "savage-continent" for pagan crown and Christ.

What was Squanto's peoples' reward
        after more sullen travelers survived?
Warrior-proud Wampanogs or Algonquins
        did not serve them like some
brown-skinned waiters and waitresses,
        happy in Pocahontas feathers
with hands eager for jive-glass bead wampum tips,
or acting Tonto phonies, "You smart, Kemo sabe,"
after sharing a thousand-year-old tradition, then to be told,
"Thanks for the popcorn chief, now head West!"

Eighteen-Holed Dreamers Gotta Go

The sooner them white-belted Johnny Carson
Arnie Palmer wannabes take their plaid outfits
with argyle socks and topless brims
to the outskirts of Aztlan and stay there,
the better it will be.

Watch 'em stand with hard drinks in their soft hands,
sticking thick brown cigars into their thin-lipped mouths,
then checking in their pastel-colored pants pockets for
their dimpled balls, to see if they're still there.

Then they pretend to tee-off with their invisible swings
hoping to hear someone's window break,
why don't they play inside, save the greens from pesticides,
and make bogies under bright halogen lights and artificial turf.

Sure, some of them dress in sweatshirts and jeans like regular
working-class stiffs, but that's when they don't wanna leave
a tip for their waitresses, bellhops or caddies who they call lazy.

What's really on their minds beyond the next flagstick hole?
Can't they see the destruction of their divot-dizzy ways,
maybe they're gonna realize there's no water left in poor
communities after an avenging angel resolves their next
move with an uzi instead of a new driving iron.

The game was meant for Scotland,
not scorching lazuli Scottsdale,

their handicap greens are cool in Cambridge or even Chicago,
not dry Arizona or rocky Colorado,
such play makes perfect sense in the Irish rains,
not amid shrinking New Mexican forests,
or along the Rio Grande Valley.
I'll go so far and say *chale* to Chi-Chi and Lee,
keep your slicings east of the Big Muddy Mississippi,
instead of using up what nourishes us.

One day all will be welcomed to the greens
of Aztlan's heights, just as long as they scale
their mighty strokes and putts to run
the maze of miniature golf.

El Comandante

Ché, they're digging up your asthmatic bones like bloodhounds,
that same circle of guerilla hunters who lived far away
from cola-cola-less Villegrande,
who now want sweet tourism dollars in the mountains,
where condors once passed above corn beer slopes,
sterilized valleys and
comatose mouths of 100 haciendas.

What will the villagers buy when golden visitors
leave behind glittering offerings and polaroids?
Will barefoot indian children praise
your former interrogator General Barrientos
as they push through a *supermercado* check out line
with bags of free trade interloper ho-hos and cheese whiz?

Their parents' faltering lungs ache,
with tracheas narrowed to drinking straws,
and nights remain cold as the Yuro ravine
where the dictator's army encountered
your ragged band of adventurers
that distant October hour of the ovens.

"Our sacrifice is for the future,"
you told seventeen *compañeros* tasting
the same defeat as the tin miners in Bolivia's dark bowels,
well before Spanish-speaking U.S. Rangers,
Ñancahuazú-trained informers, and an eye-in-the-sky satellite
transmitted your sainted rage against the machine.

Getting Closer

I reject every bulldog, fangs-
a-poppin', three-colored ace
who comes dressed for comfort in
an extra-large proletarian production,
hustling to please ya' or brow beats sya'
with his flag in your face.

Some folks flash notions of ethnicity just above
their steering wheels or by wearing sloppy slogans
across their flabby guts, thanking God for being born
Irish, but never speaking a word of Gallic, or claiming
an African matrix with their buxom corn row Cleopatra,
while thuggery baseball bunny asks, "Yo, *qué pasa?*"
Surrounded by his bat-wielding buddies in droopy
drawers stinking like ten-thousand cafeterias.

Why are there always stooges in funky hair cuts
trippin' to be blunt about nothing in particular,
do you think it's strange to see paint-sniffing,
gun-toting, flubber-faced children in the mall
looking for something hard to fill their soft skulls?

On the el, a rude gold-chained *perro*
claims two sweaty seats to sit down
and spread out his unsweetened jello-*nalgas*,
all the while complaining living in the city is like
losing a sports bet every day to monkey men with lots of money.

But he can't fool me, waggin' his wooden *maraca* of a tongue,
telling me his root country continually suffers unnatural calamities
leading to vast moral bankruptcy and dreams of narco-democracy.
Understand *pocho*head, I've lived the rural *mundo* trip,
complete with lard *papa* tacos, ringworms, steaming field work,
drafty outhouses, stale milk and unpaved streets in Texas.

Ni modo, he only knows his suffering spot on the map and snarls
with accented pride, "Ya better look out, we're coming to get cha,"
I ponder if maybe the *vato* is flying on da dope hidden under
his hip-hop-sized sumo pants or sails of his used *sombrero*.

Soon It's Robots

Smokers huddle at a thousand doors,
withdrawing 12 minutes every day
from the new-world mirage,
no one inhales the same any more,
as mosquito-mean bosses look for blood in
every dollar, expecting us to laugh to forget our stress.
Ya don't call in "sick" or expect a raise, so fragile are
job guarantees these days, that pink slips
are sent without a two-week notice or regrets
for your IDs and keys.

It's about to rain fiscal ill-will when auditors
show up in green rubber boots and umbrellas,
they'll purge the place for pro-bono fame,
to contribute to the mayor's re-election bid,
fully expecting his guano-covered ship to win.

Every Christmas your debts throb hangover hard,
followed by numb New Year reruns, waking to dark
cold coffee, back to shuffling papers and
leaving three phones unanswered.
Pete, another colleague, has gone seeking
precarious temp employment
somewhere up the street.

What don't you believe? That you'll be sacrificed
by greedy priests serving the one-eyed money moloch?
If you're smart, you won't light another match,

even if it's the white man's most ingenious planetary gift,
you see, the company is watching,
checking conversations, wastebaskets, and computer screens,
I'd say you're better off eating that damn cigarette
when your file is so thick.

Over in a glass building reflecting like a highway patrolman's
mirrored shades, manicured applause flutter
across a board room, followed by discriminating cigars
and brandy poured into crystal goblets, they close with pithy
toasts in celebration of profits after reduction in personnel.

We haven't moved a muscle but we're ripped,
hopes down-sized, and for our loyalty we're shown
the bottom line, and soon it's robots and our exit time,
to look for that phosphorus head of luminous
full-time commitment, amid crushed butts
and ashes at our feet.

It's Not the Heat, It's the Stupidity

Red stick rendezvous, we ponder raft transportation
walking to the muck's edge, who can say if fourth
of July jolly-making pyrotechnics don't prevent
this city's wharf from turning into rusty cargo?

Skin n' bones sugarcane masters have become
the sophisticated sons of muffeletta excess,
keeping their long traditions of commerce, corruption
and kickbacks, allowing two-ton barges to sail silently
with subtropical booty breaking the swamp's isolation,
bright as a Dog Star for Dixie deals and the Civil War.

On an overcast grey day, visitors
marvel at gnarled hulks of Mississippi
sassafras and shagbark hickory,
latched crab-like across metal beams and bridges,
the river is wide and blindly replenished, once
captive to gator lore and gamblers, today
it takes its liquids from simple shanty farmers
and millionaire pharmacists, still, no one white
recalls plantation fertility rites, songs of unconquered
slave night drummers, chawasha sisters and brothers,
muscles meshed in sweat, daylight branded on the back
and handed over for centuries beating past
mute liturgies laid down shoulder to shoulder,
under the sails of a jibe colossus sweeping the first
jazz piano player to cook rice and beans
for red stick's neighbor, New Orleans.

We are such frail witnesses
to an old baton rouge swollen with
blue laughter, unblinking black trains, and pier pilot flags
that flap for a commonwealth resplendent in its contradictions,
her industry's isthmus of aborted experiments encircle
the gulf's belly-filling crayfish for cajun connoisseurs who
may mock us, unaware of emergency-room reluctance,
no, they didn't feel Christ's conjured presence in
a bowl of tabasco-covered allergens when
hurricanes made our gumbo cooler.

Soil Mechanics

Tonight we'll drink sweet juice
like hummingbirds,
before we make
our prayer circle
and remember forbidden
Herculeneum,
its one hundred children
wrestling at night
in a fevered sleep,
and mothers' socket-throbbing
headaches
cycling spark plug plasma
born of lead batteries'
dark fingers of smoke.

Herculeneum, Missouri
site of lead poisoning

El Trabajo Nuevo

La voz al final
de la línea
no es la mía.

Olvida el nombre que te dí
cuando nos hablamos,
solamente entiende que de parte
de este actor durante mis horas
de solitario de nueve a cinco,
existe una necesidad real
de ganar un reporte
entusiasta.

Medio en efectivo adquirido
después de cientos de facturas
apiladas. Pues, dame esa pequeña
satisfacción en tus respuestas,
pero recuerda cualquier
comentario que hagas
se mantendrá más bien
archivado que una cinta
en las manos buscadoras
del F.B.I.

Sabes, ellos en la oficina
principal anotan todo
como los gran marcadores,
entonces si pudiera mantener

un paso estable,
me quedaría contando
las ruedas que giran, tonos de señal
en el teléfono, línea tras línea
de apellidos y códigos calientes.

Y si trueno mis dedos cansado
el supervisor fisgón gritará,
"Llame a otra persona!"

Mientras envolvemos la noche
en nuestro turno
para mejor circulación.

Spin the Bottle

Last night I encountered
two dark-haired beauties,
first a shy Chippewa,
born in Wisconsin
just off the reservation.

Many patrons seemed
to know her, they kept
calling her "Leni Couger"
or something like that,
with all the loud music and
people talking it was hard to hear.

She left the table
a few times
but always came back
refreshed and escorted by
a bartender or waitress.

Rumor had it that
her people's signature attire
started in the 1860s:
a wide red cotton headband,
a single fancy feather
jutting forward from
the knot in back,
with two thick black braids
tied in thongs of leather.

She reminded me of an Indian
woman from the Land O' Lakes region
I dated while working breakfasts
as a short-order cook.
I broke it off with that one
when I quit dairy products,
but every now and then
I see her with someone else
at the supermarket.
I kinda miss the way
she use to butter me up,
but I'm healthier without her.

The other woman at the bar
was an exciting trilingual,
commanding attention
in English, Spanish
and the language of her
Indian people–Nahuatl.
She came from Cholula,
her nickname was "Lula,"
which sounds like *chula*
which she definitely was,
perfectly dressed
in radiant *Jalisco* white,
like some 19th century
peasant's daughter,
wearing a garland of phallic-yellow,
red and green chili peppers,
I think she was showing off
just how many men she'd gotten hot,
and she almost baked *me* alive
with her fiery presence,

good thing "Leeni" was there
to keep things flowing,
but I was tempted to kiss Lula's full lips
coated in *ajo, cebolla y chili piquín*.

Hungover with retro burn kicking in,
I reminisce about the Chippewa, so satisfying,
y la Mexicana, deeply authentic,
but what kind of evening is it anyway
when you sweat crazy over labels
on bottles of beer and *salsa picante*?

Are The Tacos Taking Over?

We feasted on a hot Chinese foo-foo plate for two at the Pearl Moon Cafe in Defiance, Ohio, when I learned from *mi hijo* Camilo that San Antonio was North America's *tortilla* capital. The weight of this honor is staggering!

Simón que yes, those *pachanga* dancing *tejanas*, rolling and flattening fat flour and corn *masa*, to cook *rasquachi*-style on the stove's burner, until warm and puffy then turned over by *mano, es cierto, las mejores tortillas* are still made *en casa*.

Crystal City is another Texas town to lay claim to some food-stuff fame, "The World's Fresh Spinach Capital." It's where a six-foot statue of Popeye stood next to city hall checking on all Del Monte workers *como mi abuela María*. She packed cans of iron-rich greens in honor *de ese pelado con un ojo cerrado*, the tattooed, bow-legged, muscle-bound lover of *la flaca* Olive Oyl. He was *siempre* sucking that corncob pipe (it's amazing he didn't get lip cancer) and painted in old-fashioned colonial white.

But in the late 1960s, the *Chicanos de Cristal* turned the bigots' game around, and elected a majority leader for themselves, José Angel Gutiérrez of *el partido Raza Unida*. That's when narrow-minded Anglos left town, hoping Mexicans would soon run it down, so whites could say in their twangy way, "We told you that would happen a-me-gos." Instead, their departure was marked by high schoolers who painted the cartoon sailor a formidable shade of brown, closer to that of a sunburned field worker, then hung a sign around Popeye's anchor-thick neck, "*Somos quienes somos, y no somos sonsos!*"

What's next? Will Chicago's Latinos soon claim from sales charts in Crain's that the "windy city" is the country's leader in beans; *que frijoles* and *habichuelas* are making music together, so the racists better start treating us right or we're going to get down and organize a *pedo* night.

Beto y Oso

Oso's boss Beto Villa,
a suit-wearing south
sider had the unmistakable
air of burnt tortilla.

Oso normally liked everyone,
but was repulsed by Beto's
managerial style, which Oso
described as a cross between
riding a lubricated crocodile
and being brow beaten by a
gridiron grizzly like old coach Ditka.

In short, he was a nerve-wracking
pain *en el culo*, who felt it was his
duty to keep checking and stacking
every item in every aisle.

Beto really didn't enjoy white-knuckling
his Pay-Mart crew. On average, they were
good kids and almost 14 years his junior,
he thought all they lacked was some respect
for how good we had it in this great country.
Maybe, a little old-fashioned military discipline
might shape 'em into Chicago's
finest lamp and fixtures department.

Beto was not a Vietnam Vet,
because in the summer of '65,

he was busier
than a one-legged man in a
ass-kicking contest,
putting down political rebellion
en la República Dominicana.
Yup, that's right, Beto's line-dog skills
were earned the hard way.

Now, he was no common latrine lawyer,
field grunt, buck private,
tentpeg or C-ration snuffy.
No, his time was well spent
in the company of the few
and proud bulldog puppies.

So Beto was no mere soldier,
he was a haughty leatherneck,
a jarhead in white gloves and dress
blues, one of Uncle Sam's miserable
children—a member of the Marine Corps,
pulling embassy duty with tax-paid
caseheads loaded clips and
automatic muzzle lips.

When duty called Beto
from his "Kensington Bumtown Gents,"
he didn't have any regrets,
because he heard he'd be
stationed on an island of
Spanish-speaking fun & sun.

This was shortly after that bearded
yahoo Castro seized power and red Nikita
had promised us a nuclear shower,
but instead it was beret Ché's

plan to encircle our system with
"...two, three, many
Vietnams," which really paved
the way for other dark-eyed
rebels to torch their daddy's
sugarcane plantations and
scare off investors for
Mafia-run obligations.

Oso was a bit jealous of Beto's
adventure on exotic *Hispaniola*,
that weird hunk set down between
the Atlantic Ocean and
the Caribbean Sea,
where two Romance languages
French and Spanish,
mutated and split
like a sun-stroked coffee bean.

Oso himself rarely traveled and
felt lucky to get outside the *barrio*,
though just the thought of getting on
an airplane made him dizzy, and besides,
if he crashed in water, he couldn't swim.

Oso knew if he could get
Beto to speak
about life on military time,
then regular work would stop
for a while as Beto recounted
how he got his purple heart.
"Say *jefe*, tell us how you
cracked on the commies."

Enthusiastically Beto
signaled everyone to gather,
"*Pues jefe*, how'd it happen?"
Another *bato* asked,
"Did you ever visit Haiti?"
Then Beto crouching cat-like, conceded,
"Yeah, I got to the edge
of the zombie nation, but
I didn't go much further,
besides I don't know how to
parle vu in Creole.

"Yeah, we stalked the rebel
phantoms of the false future
barrio to barrio,
casa to casa,
mano a mano,
searching for armed
Dominican high school
and college kids who thought
they could play insurgents,
while unable to get their lazy
compatriots to join them."

Then Beto grinned his
big cheeked grin, adjusted his
glasses and dug back in,
"In less than a week,
we had them running
for the broadleaf jungle,
like commuters sprinting
for the last loop bus.

"Man, we shagged them out
to the bush, covering the

place like a thick mantilla
all the while making crap fly
through our entire half of the isla.

"We swang our forces from Puerto Plata
to the main drags of Santo Domingo,
our objectives were nearly met,
when we called on the guys over in
Haiti to lend us a crushing hand,
hell, what did they expect us
to do, agitating like broken washing
machines, going against our
international interests and
doing it so as to influence
our friends in Puerto Rico.

"I guess we could have starved them out,
but the brass wanted to build better
relations with the likes of Papa Doc Duvalier
and his vicious goons the tonton macoutes.

"So we moved in with helicopter-back
precision, as a wave of Green Berets
did their talented best, within hours,
the last rebels danced between our
bullets and Haitian machete whacks,
funny thing is, I sort of felt sorry
for the dupes we didn't capture,
because when we scoped out the results
of our border ambush,
there were a lot of headless bodies
sun-rotted like bloated ripe bananas
piled up on the back of a truck.

"Yeah, that's where I got wounded in action
and the first and last time I saw Haiti,
I sure wouldn't want to be one of those
boat refugees or Catholic left-wingers
being returned to that miserable
scaffold of a country."

Armadillo's Diagnosis

I.

Mexican kids forge a million circles,
palms wrap tightly around brightly ribboned bats,
every eye in the yard is put on guard as
gyrating sluggers are blinded then spun
before candy fireworks fly in all directions.

II.

Roosters raise a farmer to his feet,
he'll toss a ton of fresh dung on fields
for young ambitious millet, the grain of choice in China–
We aren't keen on these tiny yellow seeds,
smaller than pigeon pea pellets,
we avoid "Chino" chow
even if it might balance our blood
after devouring piñatas' rainbow treats.

III.

We splash through papier-mâché fountains,
fill rooms with las mañanitas songs
and recurring birthday wishes,
Mexicans will keep shoveling sweets
even if it causes an ache in the pancreas.

But don't listen to what Armadillo tells you,
he's never had a birthday party,
so he's jealous.

Hermanas Guapas (Pretty Sisters)

Grip June
with your thighs,
when your piece is
as big as Athens and
those pillars lasso you
into slow-stepping
cheek-to-cheek in
the unplowed moonlight.

Southern radios are tuned
to ragged royal voices sharing
a common curse and flair for whiskey,
the deep bayous are misunderstood
wetlands with an allspice marimba charm,
c'mon, you like harmonica music don't cha'?

All I wanted were some kisses, *nomás besos loca,*
pero it was the peaches *en tu boca*
that kept me from tasting those
olive Mediterranean lips.

You can live in Corpus and Houston or over
to Louisiana, where mildew grows good
and crazy if you don't make
appointments to bathe.

Now *chula*, get in the tub,
and turn on the shower,

cause if you pour water
on your lounge promise
you'll be ready to take
the last slug train out,
mounted gallantly,
hips and buttocks,
doing mileage on swine-
covered seats,
as I ride a red horse
back to the blacksmith's
house, where a naked witch
will greet me, fill a furnace
with dried coriander and okra,
pulled from the garden of
the missing Okeechobee man
who was once your lover.

The Eighth Commandment & Uranium 235

"It was Martinez, that Navajo Indian from over by Bluewater who discovered uranium, it says so in this here brochure…"
> —Simon J. Ortiz, Fight Back: For the sake of the people, for the sake of the land.

Consider how every granule was
processed for a final furious detonation
over the rising sun's bureaucracy,
where bodies burned
like Bunraku figures
and disappeared
into the burdock dark,
leaving fine glowing ash.
The memory of this assault
is rooted in the fifties' assertion
that a celestial non-stop generation
of unconfiscable electricity
would be ours forever.

Electricity so vast
that the grid authorities
linking the first world's conduits
would have us believe in its omnipresent
conspicuously cheap power, available for
mere pennies, a few coppers,
a centavo or two.

Oh yeah, what benefits we'd enjoy
by mining the burning embers,

keeping us connected to the ever-
blooming spectacle for everyone.

The resiliency of its brilliant resin
grew like aspidistra,
becoming an infernal resident
to be stashed ton after ton onto
tarp-covered 18-wheeled rigs,
heavy loaded then driven with
construction crane algebra,
to be bulldozed as beach
brine into deep-dug pits,
so thick reinforced caverns
ringed by German shepherds,
armed guards and looped over and over
razor wire, lit with a Belial charge,
makes it way off limits to inspection,
while its sealed desecrated contents
stew day after day
beneath Mescalero lands.

They say we needn't worry,
the shielded fuel is tattooed
with flashy yellow & black triangles,
a silent warning for all ages
across the widths of barrel bodies
which exteriors slowly become
the taut sandpaper
texture of deep sea sharks.

O Mako, Tiger, Hammerhead, Thresher,
O white sheath demons in the slipstream of progress,
promising no slippery barrel will ever leak,
inside the ten-fold miniaturized world

of short-sighted alchemy,
where nuclear curie scientists
have given us the fool's responsibility
to provide a permanent home
for invaders sequestered in our *Aztlan*.
Compa', I dread tomorrow knowing
que mis hijos y otros inditos y chicanitos
will be robbed by a world that designs
its resorts and golf greens by gambling
with rare water under uranium friction.

No oracle, village elder,
ace reporter or fat country commissioner
need tell us about the grey wake
these land-eating sharks make
after they've been piled one on another,
forming a catacomb of unappeased energy
locked up in foul steel-ribbed drums,
drums to beat for centuries,
interminably dangerous to *nuestra sangre*
y la madre tierra.

Simon, I wish these veins were never discovered,
below fields and valleys worked by native-dreamers
over ten-thousand summers,
and farmer ranchers who handled this soil
with respect, confident in the land's seasonal renewal,
but that was long ago, long before the sharks
headed in our direction with eyes like their makers,
eyes that never close, but instead,
continuously cast a fixed gaze
on all they will devour.

Tejas Ode

"Gentlemen, remove hats, no pictures, no refreshments."
    —sign at the entrance to the Alamo in San Antonio, Texas

Una vez, yo toqué las alas
de un zopilote tejano,
con plumaje azul y negro,
más obscuro que las montañas
de Tennessee o Virginia,
donde los voluntarios del Alamo
salieron con ojos blancos,
y pobres esclavos aherrojados
y forjados dentro el horno
americano.

Sí, ellos de rostros pensativos
y palabras fastidiosas después
de todos los tristes sermones de
cada domingo, soñar con ecos
de brindis y mentiras por mi
tierra natal.

O zopilote de luna colorada
y pinzas que cortan divinamente
el galón del cielo, yo estoy aquí,
enfrente del templo de mi primo,
el nopalero, hijo de Tenoch,
y como él, yo tengo
la tenacidad, no, la
terquedad del pimentón
crudo.

On the Bus

Sitting juicy, poppin' buttons
with prosperous bellies
filled with "sliders" and rolled-in-flour
mushroom and sweet-meat pierogis,
it's getting so your wallet
don't fit, we're still talking about
hitting the lottery with a shoe-stinky dollar,
were talking about wearing a one-size-
fits-all losing team's cap,
we're talking airport and stadium headaches
with aldermanic dough boys doing
the ghost payroll rap.

Passing streakless big-eyed windows,
sidewalks swept clear of all debris,
these old-country Poles know order,
tonight lonely guys are drinking
beer and vodka at the vinegar-stale bar
where Kracow Frank tells his wife he's at
the office on Thursday nights, not busy
wooing plump Wiggy Wierzbicki
with Alberto VO in her hair,
you know she went on a shopping spree
for toys at the Alley, she likes to get silly
in bed, and lucky dog, collected her bonus
before the Stewart Warner factory closed.

We're talking "Free Turkeys"
to the first fifty folks

who'll deposit their life-savings
in federally-insured jars,
next door at the Montrose corner store,
we're talking greens at twelve cents a "pund,"
where pigs' feet are always today's special,
we're talking sulky harnessed
horses on a Maywood track,
we're talking second generation
Polish and Spanish in the back
of a Milwaukee Avenue bus,
headed downtown at ten p.m.

Chicago's blue bagging it,
and garbage men are on strike,
Walter fell off Goldblatt's roof
without making a splat,
would you drop him a card?
When it's warm he sits outside
and listens to thirty big-band
swing recordings
made at the Blackstone.

Passing optimistic school kids
who just finished eight years
of threats and study,
yet their folks are talking
they didn't learn nothing.

Maria's eyes are war red
from the video screen all week,
she uses glasses when reading *fotonovelas*
and we're talking carpal tunnel syndrome,
her *novio* Don is on worker's comp,
he worked in Brookfield Zoo's

snake pit for more than a year
before being bit.

The guy sitting next to me wants
sympathy, he's a twenty-six-year-old
virgin looking for a Latina girlfriend,
if he suggests Tania's,
let him pick up the tab.

We're talking about some
serious depression,
the kind that crumbles
like eggless cornbread,
we're talking about the
bachelors in leather and
gang members who vote.

We're talking about
mega-malls and flea markets
where you can purchase old Tylenol
and Chinese dogs
that do birth control tricks,
we're talking about our Jefferson
Park dinner of chicken, green beans,
creamed corn, potatoes, jello salad,
and hot-buttered rolls, with the joint's
bottomless cup of senior-special coffee.

Atrocity in the Assassin/nation

I just met Mr. Pragmatic,
school-wise scholar,
he's trying to get ready for the future,
so he got himself a P-H-D-D-T
from fancy M.I.T., or did he say DeVry?

His post-industrial heart,
is chambered off from feelings
that would distract him, as he crunches big numbers
doing research on the road that would render
grave-digging obsolete.

He's never been inside a sweat lodge,
he resists superstition,
and feels closer to Marx than to God.
He's a regular dialectical materialist whose contradictions
allow him to take Bill Gates as his guide and dump Ohsawa.

Was it after Union Carbide did its Bophal, India body count?
Or when PCBs chased the folks at Love Canal out,
or the spread of airport diseases starting with HIV
when people choked on a no mañana menu.

Still, our high-paid expert want us to
prosper under techno-heaven gains,
we should be pleased with the size
of our disks and the lunch time
fever of microwaves.

Appendectomy

Can you jump from here?
There's nothing to grip on,
better use your flat footed
wide-heel bones to dig in.

Your height offers no clues
to why you're fluent in Spanish,
or why Hindus are not
mentioned in Genesis.

It's true, I didn't believe in Eden
until I met you, I sought comfort in
Patmos' visions of Apocalypse and
steaming bowls of aged miso.

Chale esa, con tu alpha y omega onda.
Tu tiempo is not my *tiempo*, you just
might say I'm doing the Yugo Tito thang,
suppressing all the differences between us,
so tomorrow's emergencies won't be my crisis,
pues, even if they were, you'd still rule *mi reina*
dulce corazoncito, making a chase scene until
lighting storms above our trained genitalia.

Who knows, we might even have a chance to
dance to "The Hero with the Thousand Faces,"
without hearing from ol' Joe Campbell, only
let's make it happen during an August sunshower.

Before we go, let's enshrine our navel embraces
when wind chimes flutter in dawn's glimmer,
then taste salty melon-seed tears as garden
clouds quench black soil with rain kisses.

I can't recall why your friend carved
headstones with the words, "I watched clouds,"
then cried thorns for his sleek doberman crushed by
the speeding car. It doesn't help me to remember
the months I slept in a burnt-out trailer like a yogi
squatter, a lonely buckwheat-filled pillow on an acrid
mattress, eating rice and raisins, while you worked for
a degree and waited tables in the shadow of Buckminster
Fuller's acorn-shaped buildings, as I hunted for your address
among the torn pages of Carbondale's telephone directory
that always smelled of patchouli.

Please don't ask me about politics,
I didn't participate last year,
or the time before, it's like the brave wobblies
say, "Dethrone your bosses' party this way,
don't vote, it only encourages them!"

Look, ninety-nine percent of the nay tion's
pollsters are lacking in simple experience,
it's mere book worship *con ellos puro saliva*,
not a pinch of practice is going on
inside those wingtips and tailored grey suits
that head downtown for needless mark-ups
and gene-splicing fat-free herb salad.

You still want opinions, how's this;
don't try to measure your tan
against the arms of an outdoor working Texan,

and Mexicans who graduate from Harvard or Yale
are still going be *pelones* if not *pendejos*,
and pound for pound, living in and around
the chain of lakes or even Lake Calumet
will give us something to drink,
when the last majestic banquet offers
the best ham off the bone in Cicero
or Toledo for that matter.

Estrellitas

Julian and Mia
sat outside
abuela's casa,
watching heaven's
sparklers hang quietly
in the bay of darkness.

Thinking they'd miss
one or a dozen
flashing tips,
falling from an
hidden angel's scepter,
each tried not to blink,
and kept their chins lifted
like moon-struck coyotes.

With sore eyes and
stiff necks they were
just about to stop,
when the top of
the vast night sky
beaded up briefly
like a woodland moccasin
then rained bright
plumed cinders.

Tochtli Luna and Cuauhtli

Once upon a time,
white clay man grew
tired of looking at the sky,
so he made a ship to lift
himself off this living sphere.

He forged the tools for far-traveling
strength to reach the nearest aureole
island floating silently above a million
terrestrial years.

Harnessing volcanic heat
under its breast this
momentous swift spear
was launched the Eagle.

Upon landing, its talons found
evidence of other two-legged people
who had left on the pocked-
marked pelt of the silver rabbit
moon, a pair of dusty handmade
leather Mexican *huaraches*.

The Gift

Taking the ceramic shoe
out of a box,
single left step,
locked in white fire glaze.
Resting on a
window sill,
it casts a silhouette
to passersby.
Close up there are five
shiny stickers cut like
valentine hearts,
in honor of missing
left toes and full foot senses.
Only a few dollars were
spent to own this
smooth, tongueless shape,
speaking a special message
understood by virgin nurses
in ghost-leg hose,
as pure high-heeled kitsch
betraying its alleged purpose
as an ashtray,
a small plant holder or
a hard candy dish.
One night it whispers
something about Cinderella,
handle with care,
looking for its fragile mate.

Premonition

Two million gnats hatch
at the edge of Africa's savannah,
four million wings rack
hurricane winds together,
to ignite a ten-day global
current coming our way
with its God-awful crescendo.

America's western shoreline,
a knock-kneed zone for slaughter
when earthquakes turn Seattle's
buildings to peanut butter.

Europe's busy knaves alight in
the Caribbean for rum and coffee,
leaving behind homicidal bees to
split Rio de Janeiro for First World
nectars, on the way whipping some
slow pokes trying to get over the
erratic Mexican U.S. border.

Penitent armadillos turn east
reaching lusty Oklahoma,
and each winter they linger a bit longer,
eventually, they'll end up in
Chicago, when palm trees start
growing in the middle of Iowa.

Pillar-eating termites join
wall board rats to ventilate
twenty-year-old housing projects,
ripe with sloth and mismanagement,
no one knows how it happened,
and silent token Sam ain't talking.

Cats rip up the last leather covered
sofas in L.A., as their pet owners
are warned about naming critters
after war heros and fat presidents.
Vegans are glad to not be feeding
from the top of the food chain,
when pigeon is the main course.

Meanwhile, Ganges' filth is still holy water,
Florida disappears into a series of sinkholes,
and sulfuric gas replaces city air when taxes
are raised for glossy color publications
that you can order, like the one on how to build
your own survival bunker from the spies at
P.O. Box, Pueblo, Colorado.

Singing Armadillo

He drove a back-to-the-island
meal ticket on wheels, brighter than
any Ohio refinery fire, and pulled
slowly into Canton's Amtrack station
with a stiff-legged hound, mounted
to the rub-a-dub cab's hood.

The driver, decked in a stripped
cat-in-the-stove-pipe-hat topping
reddish brown dreadlocks
that spilled past his lean shoulders,
looked over his green tints with a tilt.

It was his owl-route ritual
to check for travelers
from midnight to three,
my *tocayo* Cortez
and I were headed home
after the first Kenneth Patchen fest
in hard-drinking Warren.

Rasta ready, eager to deliver,
he stood relaxed in his Jamaican
birth-canal tan as he asked the
rickshaw puller's question,
"Hey mon, are ya comin' r goin'?"

Amid the dozen
suitcase snoozers camped

around the station's benches
I turned to him and answered,
"My buddy and I are word dealers
returning on the next train to Chicago,"
to which he replied,
"Well, give my regards to the splift-
smokers at the Singing Armadillo,
but I'll drive ya dare if ya writes a
poem for Ethiopia's Haile Selassie,
the Conquering Lion."

Bout to Leave the Barrio

A warm California breeze
lifts a cirrus cloud of smoldering
cigars and cigarettes, the gym's
cone lights cast spears down
where every bench is filled.

The crowd is gathered to see two
tight-lipped boxers stalk each other,
the fight is all for the spectators' pleasure,
who belch and bellow demands in
English, Spanish and Portuguese,
impatient for muscular *cholos* caged
in a dream to perform their
brown-skinned rooster routine.

Each two-legged *gallo* knows
he's a gambler taking
his chances at the
wheel.

One fighter is a *pocho* in red and gold,
he knows how to go toe-to-toe with
drunk *campesino* royalty and roughneck punks.
Barrio *cantinas* were his training grounds,
now, he wants to be a household name,
except the referee can't pronounce
"Villarreal."

Then there's the crop picker José *"Lechuga"*
Longoria in his lanky stance, robed in the green
promise of winning fast money, living proof
that crossing *el río Grande* was nothing
compared to this night's prospects.

Laced up, mouthpiece in place,
the timekeeper's bell propels
them forward, turning their
gloves into inflated lobes
of brick-colored leather.

Back and forth the boxers go
until a heliotrope of facial bruises
has blossomed in the third round.
Soon both men's gloves
are streaked with blood
and hair pomade.

In the sixth,
the ropes chafe arms and backs,
for courage, Longoria thinks of abandoning
his migrant tasks for the bright galaxy
of the ring, far
from all his mocking bosses.

Villarreal, *"nunca te aguitas,"*
he never quits, his buddies say.
Sweat covered, the hewed pugilist is
looking for his big break,
before the gallows of adulthood
bully him off to the army or
some other nit-picking job.

"Dale duro pinche lechuga!"
someone laughs,
then calling at an octave higher,
a woman in a tight white dress
offers her ocular breasts to the
fight's winner, a standing Odysseus.

This causes red and gold Villarreal
to galumph and with thunderbolt vision
launch a two-minute offensive,
to pummel Longoria,
the prune picker in green,
he wallops him inside his solar plexus,
leaving a curled-up, tired fetus
on the dirty canvas.

Loco Chuy Raps wit Tony Atole

Keep your theories out of my kitchen
if you don't want to hear me bitchin',
I know hot dogs have got red dye in 'em,
but that's my favorite carcinogen,
so go on munching away with your
bird seed habit, living on a diet
made for rabbits, just keep your
tail out of my kitchen.
Flaco, I'm no animal lover,
so don't down rap my bloody steak,
and I might try your honey-carrot cake,
I've worked hard all week, that's why
I deserve this thick ice cream shake,
so what, I'll get fat,
big deal, a few pimples,
b.s., there's no relation
between eating meat and cancer.

Mira Tony, here's my answer,
a flip bird fir thee,
you, you health store whore,
see if I care if too much protein
makes for dandruff,
or guzzling booze
might make me bald,
go on, keep your corn and beans
to your savage self,
I'll eat clean canned food
off the shelf.

Say ese, you carry brown nationalism
just a bit too far, promoting brown rice
over plain old white–
alright, I'll stop drinkin' rum and gin,
just as soon as the regular
moon tours begin,
but right now I'm on the pinche phone,
making an order for the pizza
to be mailed home,
I've had it with your macro-pedos,
you better be cool or
you'll be out like an eight-inch tie,
and if you don't use a microwave oven,
how you going to get everything hot,
using candles and a box of incense?
Tomorrow, breakfast is gonna be fried spam, eggs,
grape jam and toast, you better eat everything,
since I'm playing host.

He Still Makes House Calls

Hey Jack, it's lousy the way
everyone launches barbs
against you, it's like you're
some kinda' huckster of
darkness and not a doctor.
But does it matter
what anyone thinks?
You're not in it for the money,
it's just your answer to one
of our mortal problems.

Jack, your critics just don't understand,
you're 20 years ahead of the curve,
but didn't anyone warn you
your medical degree would be
shredded up like a Michigan
pulp paper tree?
Some say you get your kicks
from helping those in deep pain
close their eyes one last time,
Jack is there even a hypodermic
needle's drop of truth to it?

Come on, what's the point?
Summer's mosquitoes are still buzzing
and more than a dozen people have
already licked the stamp of no-return
doctor-assisted D.O.A. delivery,

while your reputation spreads
across the nation courtesy of
scandal and sneers, when people
hear the name of Jack Kervorkian.

Jack, it's not easy being an angel of mercy,
especially in an age where red beret guardian angels
get jumped on public transportation, but that's another story.

So if I may make a suggestion,
next time you think of getting
involved, try to disguise it a bit,
make it appear more like a
travel agency service and offer it as:
"Jack's Never Come Back Journeys," or
"Kevorkian's River Styx Rendezvous,"
maybe something short like,
"Terminal Travels," you get the idea.

Now here's the plan, just load your patients
into a van and drive to nearby central Detroit
or Chicago's West Side for the (last) time of their lives,
with a little effort, you can outfit them in
nifty gang colors of an opposing posse,
just be sure to deposit them in hot shot territory
looking real sporty in their big league football
or baseball uniforms of questionable distinction,
add that special turn of the brim and a dozen arcane hand signs
known as an inner-city lexicon to be practiced in open-air splendor.

Then soon out of a car's dark window,
at an oblique angle a locally antagonized shooter
will show you and your death-wish patients
how to go down under a lenitive hail of bullets,

I'll admit, it's not totally meticulous
like your machine,
but with a fast pass of one urban uzi
aimed just so, they won't know what hit them.

Jack, think of the possibilities,
the authorities would never blame you,
'cause you're no gang-banger,
Jack, this kind of thing
happens here everyday,
and the controversy
quickly blows over.

Jack, this could be the answer,
Jack, are you listening?

Our Evil Empire

*In the summer of 1965, African-Americans
in Los Angeles Watts district rioted for eleven days.
A total of 35 deaths were reported.*

There are times
when our city becomes
America's Beirut on the lake,
like that hot August weekend
when ambulances rushed
as if war had been launched
at the close of Friday's
six o'clock news.

Just who put out the call
so many would have to mourn
across the stretch of the city?
Because more people were killed,
collected and carried off,
wrapped in stained body bags,
in less time than it took
to uproot the plotters
who staged the coup
against Gorbachev's
fading superpower rule.

While the dead are grieved,
washing away their
wasted blood
will go faster

than forgetting
all the life inside
sons and daughters,
sisters and brothers,
husbands and wives,
enemies and friends,
relatives and strangers,
that was stolen by
planned and spontaneous
acts of violence.

50 victims,
50 victims in one weekend,
some fell in stop-motion pose,
others squirmed and gasped
after the barrel-size blasts
went from Friday to Sunday.

Some people hid their kids
inside bathtubs to deflect
incoming strays,
some people lied to themselves
saying it was o.k.
to stay inside all day–
from the earliest rays
to the dark dream glow
of electrical starlight,
how many youngsters dashed past
unboarded windows
when weapons erupted and
lead sprayed across
the width of crowded projects,
parks and streets,
making it a life-or-death choice

for parents to go get
milk at the store,
as the reverberating voice
that filled the air
forced dozens to hunker
down alongside the absent sun
as more cracks of guns found another
to be laid out cold
naked toe-tagged at the morgue.

Aren't you sick
of aftermath reports–
where the guy
with the tie
stands outside the
coroner's door,
loosens his collar,
and all he can say is,
"Motives are being sought..."

But you know what,
there'd be national guardsmen
hunting down the killers
if even a quarter of
those being shot
lived in lily-white
Winnetka.

Estás Invitado y

It's September, y Marta is
serving greasy hot chicken
in red chile broth,
you won't find this meal
on some fast food menu,
this is *comida* cooked slow
like the growth of a *saguaro*.

This dish stands up
even without a *cumpleaños*
party two-candle cake,
or two full *piñatas* about
to break, what I'm saying
is this is something that
is good twice in a row,
it has sustaining powers
that are *casi indio* the way
it feeds traveling musicians,
successful city architects,
psychically-drained uncles,
and babysitting neighbors.
It's been known to take the
crick out of a working momma's
back and prevent a *viejo*'s
heart attack—this meal
was served in blue bowls,
nothing fancy, except the
way everything mixed together

with gossipy radish, dutiful
oregano and watery-lipped
lechuga simmering in a good
serving of Marta's hot
chicken in red chile broth,
that lift appetites amid
an assortment of *tamales*,
cerveza and three dozen
tortillas de maiz.

Overhead, above *nuestros cantos*,
wild *pájaros* prepare to wing
from Midwest skies *y lagos*,
taking as their only compass
last year's winter-nest impressions,
back to where earth stays vital longer
and the wind is southern sweet
far from our raincoat summer,
where we eat on top of wine-
colored cloth as our bag of sliced
limes spurt trails from their green
skin to dash tart over *pollo bien
cocido en el abrazo de cebolla*,
the ahh of *ajo*, teamed up *con*
muscular hominy disguised as bits
of shrimp speckled with
gastral-tickling *jalapeño y ancho*
placing a fire in everybody's belly.

Rumor had it that Marta, a nationalist boxing fan,
sent a large container of her special *pozole* to
Mexico's Julio César Chávez two hours
before he fought Puerto Rico's gold lover
Macho Camacho, Chávez had two bowls
and was able to knock the *sazón* out of that man.

Armadillo's Aquí Buey of Knowledge

I.
Armadillo *era carpintero*,
his back bore scars from
nails and screws after
hammering into dark spots,
his *brazos* were hard
from swacking,
with wrists a pylon of tendons,
carpentry built his *cuerpo*,
the only parts missing
were two bottom teeth,
he called it having a
"hockey-slapped smile."

Armadillo shared an apartment
with his *brujo* brother Oso,
their social lives sagged
from years of living
in bachelor clutter,
there were times when Armadillo
considered moving out
to the country with a friend or lover.

Armadillo hauled tools
in his car's trunk, he had everything
needed to "do the do,"
without spending a buck.
Oso said, "You got to be

really organized when
you're a job floater."

II.
Oso's court date finally came,
he had waited so long for that day,
"Remember the blond assailant?
Well he's bald now."

It's been a few years
of trial date postponements,
since his fight in the bar that started
when he told his bro' Armadillo,
"*Esa ruca's nalgas están bien apretadas
en las jeans que yo puedo leer las letras
sobre las mechas* in her right pocket."

The neighborhood blonde ape was in full range
of Oso's comment and in less time then it takes
to scarf an emergency taco, the tavern's *puertas*
flung open taking *los chingazos* outside,
where barely-starting-to-shave wannabe gangsters
flipped coins to see who would end up *en la cárcel*.

Armadillo jumped in and broke it up,
he didn't care for those buzzards too lazy
to tear the tags off their baseball caps
or fancy-ass gym shoes,
he had enough hard work and early morning
obligations to keep him out of most trouble.
Most trouble, not involving women.
He never got over his big-nose girlfriend,
the gypsy, Minerva, who caught him cheating.

He tried not to, but he was always found
talking to the woman whose boyfriend
or husband had just stepped away for a minute,
this excited his sense of adventure,
the Spanish pirate in him from six grandfathers ago
still sailed in his land-locked veins,
stealing moments with a fair maiden,
and a mug of grog to egg him on
to the four stages of tequila.

III.
In the first stage he'd say,
"*Sentirse rico*, I feel rich,
everybody looks so rich,"
and in the second stage he'd say,
"*Pues soy tan* good looking, yes,
I know what they're thinking, *él es bien guapo*."
Then going deep into the third stage,
"You know what, you know what?
sabes qué, I'm bulletproof *vato!*"
Después de eso, into the fourth
plano he'd get kinda ticked off and say,
"Hey, *de punta a punta*, now I'm invisible."

Glossary

conjunto–musical group often playing in Texas Mexican clubs, bars, parks, etc.

salsa–literally "sauce," meaning in musical terms the sort of Afro-Latino sound

Texaztlan–contraction of "Texas" and the Nahuatl word for the U.S. Southwest, "Aztlan"

Superbarrio–Mexico City's costumed character in a bright ski mask who mocks officials

Brown Berets–a militant Chicano youth group with chapters in the U.S; big in the sixties

chingazos–blow with the hand, fist fight

Tonantzin-Guadalupe–a combination of the Nahuatl pre-Spaniard term for "mother earth goddess spirit" that was later supplanted by a Spanish colonial Catholic icon, "Our Lady." The patron saint of the Americas, this brown-skinned holy virgin appeared in 1531 at Tepeyac, Mexico.

perro–dog

nalgas–ass, buttocks

vato–"guy" or "dude" in pachuco slang

ni modo–no big deal

ajo, cebolla y chili piquín–garlic, onion and chile

salsa picante–hot spicy sauce

mi hijo–my son

pachanga–good-time party

rasquachi–low-class, untidy

es cierto–it's true

como mi abuela–like my grandmother

de ese pelado con un ojo cerrado–of that bum with an eye shut

la flaca–the skinny one

el partido Raza Unida(LRUP)–literally, the "United People" or "Race Party." It was a third-party movement in American politics inspired and sustained by Chicanos seeking political self-determination for the Mexican Americans and other Latinos. Founded by José Angel Gutierréz, the party aim was to gain political votes in city or country areas where Chicanos were a majority.

somos quienes somos, y no somos sonsos–we are who we are, and we aren't dumb, pun on Popeye's, "I (y)am what I (y)am."

habichuelas–Puerto Rican's word for "beans"; also string beans

pedo–"fart" or a "ruckus"

jefe–literally "chief"; affectionate term for parent

nomás besos loca–just kisses, crazy girl

que mis hijos y otros inditos y chicanitos–that my children and other little Indians and Chicanos

nuestra sangre y la madre tierra–our blood and mother earth

Ohsawa–Japanese founder of modern Macrobiotic movement, author Georges Ohsawa

chale esa, con tu alpha y omega onda–(used only as interjection) No way gal, with your alpha and omega trend of the moment

tu tiempo–your time

mí reina dulce corazoncito–my queen, little sweet heart

wobblies–members of the Industrial Workers of the World I.W.W. union

pelón–skinhead, difficult person, slang for former Mexican president Carlos Salinas de Gortari

pendejo–pretender, claims to not know something, an ignoramus or jerk *con ellos puro saliva*–with them it's all talk

Tochtli–"rabbit" in Nahuatl, one of Mexicos' major pre-conquest languages

Cuauhtli–"eagle" in Nahuatl

huaraches–pre-Spanish native-made sandals worn for generations by men and women in Mexico

tocayo–anyone with your same first name

cholos–pejorative term in California for Mexican immigrants, also gang members

gallo–rooster

pocho–pejorative term for a Mexican born in the U.S., less pejorative when used by Chicanos

cantinas–bars, taverns

lechuga–lettuce

nunca te aguitas–you never give up

Dale duro pinche… –Give it to him hard damn...

Chuy–Jesús (nickname)

cumpleaños–birthday

viejo's–an old man's or husband's

cerveza–beer

tortillas de maiz–corn tortillas

nuestros cantos–our songs

pájaros–birds

y lagos–and lakes

pollo bien cocido en el abrazo de cebolla–chicken well cooked in the embrace of onion

pozole–hominy-based soup

sazón–seasoning popular in Puerto Rican dishes

brujo–male witch

oso–bear

Esa ruca's…–That dame's ass is so tight in those jeans I can read the letters on the matchbook

en la cárcel–in jail

puertas–doors

de punta a punta–from head to toe